AF225759

My Poetry Trip Through Recovery

My Poetry Trip through Recovery

A Cancer Recovery Journey with God

DIANE PARKHURST

RESOURCE *Publications* · Eugene, Oregon

MY POETRY TRIP THROUGH RECOVERY
A Cancer Recovery Journey with God

Resource Publications
An Imprint of Wipf and Stock Publishers
199 W. 8th Ave., Suite 3
Eugene, OR 97401

www.wipfandstock.com

PAPERBACK ISBN: 978-1-6667-6001-9
HARDCOVER ISBN: 978-1-6667-6002-6
EBOOK ISBN: 978-1-6667-6003-3

01/13/23

My family and friends who were praying for me
and helping me through this entire journey.

He heals the brokenhearted and binds up their wounds.

—Ps 147:3

CONTENTS

Contents

ACKNOWLEDGEMENTS

My prayer warriors

INTRODUCTION

Hello! My name is Diane Parkhurst and this is my second book of poetry. My first book was entitled My Poetry Trip Through Cancer, which I wrote while going through the diagnosis and surgery for pancreatic cancer. God gave me poetry through the journey of pancreatic cancer, and He continued to give me poetry through my recovery. I had the Whipple surgery which is quite a difficult recovery. The doctor opened me from my breastbone to underneath my navel. It took nine and a half hours to complete. I was in PICU for five days, which is a short time for this surgery. I was up and walking the same day I had surgery. It is difficult. In addition to this recovery, I was having repeated hospitalizations for kidney stones and pancreatitis. Both issues are painful! Through it all, God was with me, either by His peace given to me through prayer or by His servants He would send to physically take care of me. He was there! This book is a collection of poetry written while going through this recovery journey! I pray this book will help you through whatever journey you are experiencing.

IN YOUR PRESENCE

I wrote this because I was feeling discouraged while relearning my new way of eating and my new digestive process. When you have this surgery called the Whipple, it completely changes the way you digest your food. You take for granted just sitting down to have a meal. Everything has to be thought through before you eat. I just wanted God's help.

The Lord is with me; He is my helper. I will look in triumph on my enemies. Psalm 118:7

As I close my eyes
I see Your face
You are breathtaking
And full of grace

As I seek Your presence
I pray you forgive
Me of my sins and
Let me live

As I ask for help
Show me Your ways
And help me be more
Like You every day

As I rise to seek You
Help me see Your will
Keep me steady
And help me be still

A DIFFERENT CHRISTMAS

I wrote this during the Christmas season because I was beginning the recovery from my surgery. Usually, at Christmas, I am the one doing all the cooking and planning. This was one way Christmas was different because my family stepped in and cooked everything while I watched. My husband, David, sons, David and Daniel, and daughter-in-law, Kayla all cooked. It was great. It was also different because I definitely had a more laid-back Christmas!

She will give birth to a son, and you are to give Him the name Jesus, because He will save His people from their sins. Matthew 1:21

It was a different Christmas
Than any I had before
Nothing felt the same
And yet I had much more

My body was healing
From surgeries and such
My heart was healing as well
As I let go of any grudge

I saw through new eyes
The blessing before me
As I watched my friends and family
Who all were caring for me

I realize just how much
Who I love mean to me
And God was working through them
Each one for my eternity

So now I pray my sight
Will continue to see God's plans
To love all others well
And to rely on His wonderful plan

BRING ME BACK

God gave me this poem after I had to go to the Emergency Room in Midland, Texas because I had pancreatitis. I thought the pancreatitis was over with the cancer removal. The pain was excruciating with pancreatitis. The hospital sent me home with pain medications. This was the beginning of my delays in writing my first book and creating my blog. It is easy for satan to use fear to torment you when going through trouble. God reminded me that He is always with me!

For God did not give us a spirit of timidity, but a spirit of power, of love and of self-discipline. 2 Timothy 1:7

Lord don't let me
Go through this stress alone
Bring me back to You
When I start to roam

Fear strips me of happiness
And always causes me
To wonder where You are
And worry about everything

My soul can start to wander
And leave You far behind
When this fear comes calling
It leaves thoughts unkind

LOSS FOR WORDS

The recovery was hard. I have a large incision beginning at my breastbone down past my belly button, and I was dealing with pancreatitis. It was suggested at this point that I may have chronic pancreatitis, which left me devastated. I was feeling self-pity starting to rise in me and then, as usual, God rescued me from my thoughts.

He gives strength to the weary and increases the power of the weak. Isaiah 40:29

This recovery is hard
And I am very weak
I feel I can't go on
Relief is what I seek

I am tired of hurting
And fighting this pain
I want it all to go away
I feel it's all been in vain

They say it's chronic
And I have had enough
Of the hurt and heartache
I am really not that tough

I thought it would be over
When this surgery was done
And now I find out
There could be more to come

I am at a loss for words
And at a loss for peace
I know I have God and He
Will make all this cease

LORD WHY ME

I was still feeling the sting of the possible diagnosis of chronic pancreatitis. I was crying out to God for help. He gave me this poem.

The righteous cry out, and the Lord hears them; He delivers them from all their troubles. Psalm 34:17

Lord why me
I want to know
Haven't I been given
Enough sorrow

Lord why me
I want to understand
I am not as strong
As You think I am

Lord why me
And He replied
You will be strong enough
With Me by your side

RELEASE THIS GRIP

I felt weak in my body and weaker in my faith. I was seeking God's guidance and help because I had gone again to the emergency room, but this time it was for kidney stones. I know this was satan delaying the plans God had for me. When you are in the throes of battle, it is hard to see the victory God has for you! But God comforted me, as always!

Answer me when I call to you, O my righteous God. Give me relief from my distress; be merciful to me and hear my prayer. Psalm 4:1

The fear is real
And so very hard
It grips my body
It leaves me starved

For some kind of sign
Relief from You God
Help me understand
Where You are Lord

I can't see You
For only pain I know
No glimpse or promise
Only a dim tomorrow

Fear has me tightly
In its strong grasps
Not giving me peace
Just feeling its wrath

Oh Lord I cry
Please relieve me of this
I need Your presence
To release this grip

8

CARRY ON

God gave me energy and hope this day. I know He has a purpose for me, and this helped me so much!

For we are God's workmanship, created in Christ Jesus to do good works, which God prepared in advance for us to do. Ephesians 2:10

The devil's grasp is tight
And I feel he has delayed
The work I need to do for God
And for a moment he has dissuaded

But my God is King
And His plan is the best
He will not let the devil
Put His plans to rest

Strength God has restored
To me His lowly servant
To carry on His will and to
Continue in His service

GOD IS WITH ME

I had another kidney stone that I was able to pass on my own with pain medication. If this wasn't so painful, it would be funny. Satan always loved to attack me at my weakest, which was usually at night. God always was there encouraging me through it and promising me deliverance.

"Get behind me satan! You are a stumbling block to me; you do not have in mind the things of God, but the things of men." Matthew 16:23

There was a time
I was taken by fear
I was all by myself
With nobody near

I had terrible dreams
That caused me unrest
And I felt I was letting
My soul be possessed

The next time fear
Stood in front of me
I looked right at it
And said my God is with me

SMALL GESTURES

I wrote this for all the people who texted, called, sent cards and prayed for me. I was so grateful for the encouragement. It always was in God's perfect timing.

Therefore, as God's chosen people, holy and dearly loved, clothe yourselves with compassion, kindness, humility, gentleness and patience. Colossians 3:12

Just a small gesture
Can be overlooked
It won't matter you think to yourself
And satan has you hooked

Don't believe his lies
That small kindness doesn't matter
Because it can be huge
To someone who is shattered

Next time you feel the urge
To hug someone you know
Or send a card of concern
To a person with trouble

Don't discount or dismiss
What God tells you to do
It may seem so small
But to someone it is huge

CLOSER TO YOU

This was my continued prayer while going in and out of the hospital for pancreatitis and kidney stones. I had genetic testing done at MD Anderson because this can all be related to a thyroid condition. I was praying it was not because it could be passed to my children and grandchildren. It was not genetic.

Be still, and know that I am God. Psalm 46:10

My Father come close
Let me rest my head
On Your shoulders and breathe
Your breath of life instead of dread

My Father bring me back
Don't let me walk away
From Your loving arms
Come close to me and stay

My Father wrap me
In Your arms and help me
Be still in Your presence
And stay in Your safety

My Father teach me how
To navigate through
This life by Your side
Never leaving You

DAILY STRUGGLE

This was a dark point. I was having a really hard time understanding why God was letting me go through all the medical troubles. It was so much pain all the time and after a cancer diagnosis and major surgery, it was hard to grasp.

Consider it pure joy, my brothers, whenever you face trials of many kinds. James 1:2

Sometimes I don't want to be in this life
I just want to go away
I want to be with my Lord
And stop living this way

I'm tired of the pain I feel
And exhausted from the fight
I don't want to stay here anymore
I want to feel peace in the light

I am struggling daily
With my body and mind
Trying to heal and be whole
And that is hard to find

But it escapes me every day
And leaves me disillusioned
Seeking this new existence
And causing so much confusion

Lord lead me through this valley
I feel its dark and very sad
I need a new sense of hope
To give me the life I had

WEARY

I was exhausted from the constant fighting with the ailments. God encouraged me with this poem.

They will soar on wings like eagles; they will run and not grow weary, they will walk and not be faint. Isaiah 40:31

My body is weary
From fighting each day
Trying to recover
And remain unafraid

It is difficult to see tomorrow
I am so focused on this disease
Relying on myself to relax
Does not come with ease

Everyone says I will be okay
I am still not that sure
That this is true but
I am praying God has the cure

EVERLASTING CARE

Anytime I was feeling alone, scared, or anxious, God would always come to my rescue—either by words or by sending someone to minister to me.

Cast all your anxiety on Him because He cares for you. 1 Peter 5:7

Lord I know You will
See me through it all
You will never leave
Or let me fall

You will come and
Make sure I am alright
Every single day
And even in the night

You will reassure me
Of Your everlasting care
Never wanting me
To feel alone or scared

BEAUTIFUL THINGS

When I had a reprieve from all my illness, I was able to see the beautiful things around me. Sometimes it is hard to appreciate them when you don't feel well. I pray I pay attention to them in the future.

The heavens declare the glory of God; the skies proclaim the work of His hands. Psalm 19:1

These beautiful things
That God gives to us
The smell of a rose
And a mother's touch

The love of a Father
That heals every pain
The hummingbird in spring
And the sound of rain

The feel of a fire
When frigid weather appears
The call from a friend
When sadness is here

These beautiful things
That God gives to us
I am so thankful for how
He shows us His love

HELP ME FATHER

When I am sick, I can forget to think of others. This was my prayer to remind me even when I don't feel well to pray and think of others first.

This is my command: love each other. John 15:17

Father show me
Your will today
Let me see
The need I pray

Point out to me
The ones in pain
Keep me from spending
My day in vain

Let me hear
The cries You do
And show me those
Who need You too

Help me love others
More each day
Putting myself last
And You first I pray

EVERY HOUR EVERY DAY

God showed me so many ways He cared for me during my recovery. Whatever need I had, He would meet it. He was, and is, with me every hour and every day. I will forever sing His praises!

I will praise You, O Lord my God, with all my heart; I will glorify thy name forever. Psalm 86:12

Father open my heart
To hear what You say
The truths You share with me
Every hour every day

Tell me which path to take
And walk with me along the way
Keeping my eyes on You
Every hour every day

Share with me Your sight
To see those led astray
Let me be Your beacon
Every hour every day

Father help me understand
The dreams You've given me I pray
And let me glorify You
Every hour every day

MY HEART

I was doing the hard recovery work of walking and eating even though I felt like doing neither of those things. Whatever I had to do, I had to do with God, or I would not do it. God took care of me. I want my desires to be the same as His desires. I want my heart to match His heart.

The poor will see and be glad—you who seek God, may your hearts live! Psalm 69:32

When I am away from You
My heart isn't the same
It aches for something more
Of what I can't quite name

My heart yearns for more
Of the peace You give to me
When I am praying before the throne
It is Your face that I see

The love I seek to feel
Is just a breath away
I am asking for You to fill me
With a peace that is here to stay

BREATH OF LIFE

Every breath was precious, and every day was precious. I wrote this because I did not want to take for granted God and all He had done and all He had left for me to do.

The Spirit of God has made me; the breath of the Almighty gives me life. Job 33:4

Father remind me
Of how much I need
Your breath of life
Living inside of me

Let me see Lord
That I am hopeless
Without You with me
I lose Your focus

Fill me Oh Lord
With Your love and power
Calling me out when
I start to cower

Lord let me rise
Each day I have
To love everyone
And show them Your path

COME CLOSE

Whenever I would feel far from God, I knew it was me leaving Him. He never leaves us or forsakes us. He loves us and wants the best for us. For all I was going through, I know God had a plan and would use it for His good.

For I am convinced that neither death nor life, neither angels nor demons, neither the present nor the future, nor any powers, neither height nor depth, nor anything else in all creation, will be able to separate us from the love of God that is in Christ Jesus our Lord. Romans 8:38–39

Come close my Redeemer
Save me from this fight
Do not let me leave You
Keep me by Your side

Come close to me my Teacher
Let me learn from You today
Open my heart and soul
And teach me Your ways

Come close to me my King
For before Your throne I stay
Seeking Your forgiveness
For the times I go astray

Come close to me my Immanuel
For You are always with me
Going before me and
Caring for me completely

HOW SWEET IT IS

I wrote this one day when I was feeling so much better. I had several days of feeling good and feeling thankful I did. God gives me grace when I don't feel well, and I am thankful.

For it is by grace that you have been saved, through faith—and this not from yourselves, it is the gift of God—not by works, so that no one can boast. Ephesians 2:8–9

How sweet it is
To be known by You
To have You near me
Persevering whatever ensues

How sweet it is
To have You present
When I am at my worst
You chase away discontent

How sweet it is
To be loved by You
No matter what I say
No matter what I do

I NEED YOU FATHER

The struggle I have with my stomach is real and I could not endure it without my Father! It makes me realize on my worst and best days how much I need His help.

I can do everything through Him who gives me strength.
Philippians 4:13

I need You Father
When my world is falling
When I don't have any answers
To the questions that keep calling

I need You Father
When trouble is at my door
Relentlessly knocking
Shaking me to the core

I need You Father
When fear fights against me
Filling me with doubts
And only distress I see

I need You Father
To draw me close to You
I need to feel Your presence
In everything I go through

A VALLEY

I wrote this during my recovery. A month after surgery, I began passing kidney stones. During January, I had two trips to the emergency room and two procedures to remove kidney stones. I felt that satan was trying to hinder the work God wanted me to do with this poetry. I hope you can relate to this poem and realize how much God wants to help us!

Even though I walk through the valley of the shadow of death, I will fear no evil; for you are with me, your rod and your staff, they comfort me. Psalm 23:4

Father I'm in a valley
I can't find my way
I've tried everything
And I keep going astray

I'm out of hope
And out of energy
I need some direction
To help uplift me

I've tried it on my own
Without much success
And all I have now
Is self-induced stress

Help me my Father
To get through this place
That has me confused
And losing this race

BEACON

I was thinking of my dark days and am thankful God brings me back to His light and joy. Some people do not have His light and joy. This world can be so dark for so many hopeless people. I pray God will shine through all His people to give others hope.

For you were once darkness, but now you are light in the Lord. Live as children of light. Ephesians 5:8

My Saviour fill me
With Your Holy Spirit
Let me be a beacon in this
World so dark and desperate

Let all Your children
Shine Your light so bright
That others will have no choice
But to see the light

NOT DONE YET

I wrote this poem in the midst of my journey after a friend of mine told me, "You are not done yet." Those words inspired this poem. I think this applies to all of us in every stage of life. We are never done until we hear the verse below from our Saviour.

Well done, good and faithful servant! Matthew 25:21

My life is not over
I am not done yet
God has great plans
That don't include regret

God knows my future
He cares so much
About every detail
Everything I touch

He sees my dreams
And He lets me know
There is a lot more to do
And a long way to go

BRING ME BACK LORD

During this journey, I could wander from God. He would always bring me back.I am nothing without God.

Submit to God and be at peace with Him; in this way prosperity will come to you. Job 22:21

Bring me back Lord
When I go astray
Help me return
To Your redeeming way

Bring me back Lord
When I lose sight
Of Your plan for me
And of Your light

Bring me back Lord
When I feel distressed
And desperate for comfort
Searching for rest

Bring me back Lord
I pray for Your favor
I ask You to stay near
And don't let me waiver

REJOICE

I wrote this after I was able to return to my regular barre workout class. God had brought me through so much and I felt so overjoyed and thankful for His healing!

Be joyful always! 1 Thessalonians 5:16

God I pray
You hear my voice
When I praise You
And when I rejoice

God I pray
You give me peace
That will fill my soul
And my joy will never cease

God I pray
I remember You
And show Your love
In all I do

LORD TAKE MY LIFE

I always have the best intentions to do God's will! Sometimes I forget to ask God what His will is and what He wants me to do.

Do not conform any longer to the pattern of this world, but be transformed by the renewing of your mind. Then you will be able to test and approve what God's will is-His good, pleasing and perfect will. Romans 12:2

Lord take my life
And use it as You wish
Let me always be
A willing participant

Lord take my gifts
You have given me
To help build Your kingdom
So others can see

Lord take my sins
Far from this soul
And show me the way
That I should go

Lord take my heart
And fill it with kindness
Letting others see You
Even if they are blinded

Lord take my life
Until I breathe no more
Then take me home
To be with You evermore

DON'T FEAR

I wrote this after my quiet time because I was so worried and anxious about something completely out of my control. God calmed me, as He had done throughout my recovery, with His words. This verse is a constant go to for me because I tend to be a worrier.

Look at the birds of the air; they do not sow or reap or store away in barns, and yet your heavenly Father feeds them. Are you not much more valuable than they? Who of you by worrying can add a single hour to his life? Matthew 6:26–27

Don't fear whatever
This day may bring
Don't worry about
Anyone or anything

He cares for the birds
And you mean so much more
Just turn to Him
He is your greatest mentor

He promises to be there
No matter what troubles come
He will never leave you
The battle is already won

BE STILL AND BREATHE

I still have good days and bad days when it comes to my digestive
health. This poem is my reminder to myself to look to God, be still
and take a breath. This poem is for those having troubles.

Be still, and know that I am God. Psalm 46:10

Know God is with you
Be still and breathe
Look on His face and
Know He will never leave

Trust in the Lord
To stand and deliver
You from this fight
Leaving enemies to quiver

Stand on His word
And know it to be true
He chases our enemies
In fervent pursue

He will not give up
Nor will He ever quit
Protecting and loving you
Until the very end

HELP ME MY GOD

I woke this morning with this poem. Last week was a difficult one for me, but God delivered me. I did not feel good and I was concerned about certain health issues. I just want to put this out there, it is okay not to feel okay. I pray that if you are in sadness, God will deliver you! He will deliver you!

But you, OLord, be not far far from me. O my Strength; come quickly and help me. Psalm 22:19

My heart is troubled my God
It needs Your attention
Sadness cloaks me
In fearful desperation

My eyes are wet my God
From tears flooding through
An outpouring of my soul
That can only be healed by You

My mind is racing my God
And struggling in every way
It's asking many questions
Causing me to be afraid

Come help me my God
To defeat this invisible foe
Bring me back to Your safety
Never again leaving Your fold

SUFFERING

If I am being honest, I hate suffering of any kind. I have had my share through this recovery. I also have several auto-immune diseases that affect me daily. It is hard to understand why when you are going through it. My attitude can be the worst when I am suffering. It is only when I totally rely on God that I can have peace while suffering. I know God will use it all for good! I also love that He will restore us when the suffering is over, "making us strong, firm and steadfast." So remember whatever suffering you may be going through, God will deliver you out of it stronger than before!

And the God of all grace, who called you to His eternal glory in Christ, after you have suffered a little while, will Himself restore you and make you strong, firm and steadfast. 1 Peter 5;10

Suffering can lead us
On a path of significance
Or suffering can take
Us from God and being obedient

Event though suffering
Can be lonely and difficult
It can also be helpful
And God's miracles can result

If we call on our Father
While we go through tribulation
He will use all of it
To give us inspiration

JESUS HAS THIS

God gave me this poem today because, for a moment, I lost focus on Him and started fretting about things out of my control. He reminded me that He has got me covered. Jesus has this!

But if we walk in the light, as He is in the light, we have fellowship with one another, and the blood of Jesus Christ, His Son, purifies us from all sin. 1 John 1:7

So your heart is sad
And you don't feel bliss
Don't give up
Because Jesus has this

Your pain is great
And you feel distressed
Don't give up
Because Jesus has this

Your soul is weary
And you're not your best
Don't give up
Because Jesus has this

Your mind is full
Of worry and regret
Don't give up
Because Jesus has this

Look at the King
Because HE knows your wish
Praise and thank Him
Because Jesus has this

MY ONLY HOPE

I know I have said this before but I am a worrier. You think I would learn, right?! I know better, I know God has my back, and yet I still worry when all I have to do is give it to Him!

My hope comes from the Lord, the Maker of heaven and earth.
Psalm 121:2

You are my only hope
Who can truly calm me down
My heart seeks You Lord because
You are the only peace around

You are my only hope
When my anxiety comes to stay
You are the only answer
That can make it go away

You are my only hope
When fear knocks at my door
You are the one who knows
How my faith to restore

You are my only hope
When satan tells me lies
You always intervene
Whenever You hear my cries

NOTHING ON MY OWN

I wrote this after reading James. Chapter 3. I cannot go through cancer, recovery, daily activities or anything on my own.

But the wisdom that comes from heaven is first of all pure; then peace-loving, considerate, submissive, full of mercy and good fruit, impartial and sincere. James 3:17

I am flawed
Of this I am aware
Only with God's guidance
My troubles can I bear

My wisdom is not my own
It's given by my Lord
And only with Him
Can I see it all unfold

My life is not my own
It belongs to a higher power
Only God can show me
How everything will transpire

STEALING MY JOY

When I was writing my first book, My Poetry Trip Through Cancer, I was stressed because I wanted everything perfect. Not everything is perfect, only God. My sister, Jan, told me, "Diane, you have had cancer. This is so small in the scheme of things." Amen, sister, amen.

"Get behind me, satan!" He said. "You do not have in mind the things of God, but the things of men." Mark 8:33

I'm letting satan
Steal all my joy
He is playing with my emotions
Like his own personal toy

The good God gave me
Disappeared in a second
Because I let satan
Change my perspective

So now I say no
To satan and his plan
I know I'm not perfect
And I know who I am

I am God's child
So I'll live in His light
Not in the chaos
Of satan's plight

IT DOESN'T MATTER

I love that God loves me no matter what my sins are. Even when I continue to worry or be afraid or angry, He understands and forgives me. He is my Father and Romans 8:39 says nothing can separate me from His Love.

Neither height, nor depth, nor anything else in all creation, will be able to separate us from the love of God that is in Christ Jesus, our Lord. Romans 8:39

It doesn't matter
What your sin is
God won't leave you and
He will always forgive

It doesn't matter
As long as you seek
God's forgiveness for
When you are weak

It doesn't matter what
You did in your past
God still loves you and will
Give you peace that lasts

It doesn't matter
If you can't forgive yourself
Stay close to God and He
Will remove all your guilt

REMEMBER

When going through recovery, I found it was important to remember all the things God had done for me in the past. He keeps His promises. I think it is important that we remember God's goodness in our lives rather than dwell on the bad things in our lives. This past year has taught me this lesson. God has been so good to me this year and every year!

I will remember the deeds of the Lord; yes, I will remember your miracles of long ago. Psalm 77:11

Remember the blessings that
God has bestowed
How much He has protected me
And kept me in His fold

Remember the reason why
God allows my mistakes
So I can tell others about Him
Who are experiencing the same

Remember the answers that
God has graciously given
To desperate pleas sent
On my behalf to heaven

Remember and never forget
How much God loves me
And the plans He has
For my future I cannot yet see

AMAZING GRACE

Every day God has been with me and provided me with His amazing grace!

The grace of our Lord was poured out on me abundantly, along with the faith and love that are in Christ Jesus. 1 Timothy 1:14

How amazing is our Lord's love
He answers every prayer
Always knowing what we need
All the time and everywhere

Never is He stingy
With the care He bestows
Down to every detail of our lives
Perfect love every day He always shows

He goes before us every day
Setting our paths in place
Knowing what each child needs
And showing amazing grace

ONLY YOU

God is the only one who can restore me. I wrote this after a bout with pneumonia. He restored me so that I could go to my check up at MD Anderson!

Restore us, O God; make Your face shine on us, that we may be saved. Psalm 80:3

When trouble seeks me
I run to You Lord
You are my warrior
And so much more

When darkness consumes
And takes me hostage
It's only You Lord
Who can free me from this

When my eyes
Are full of tears
It's only You Lord
Who can calm my fears

When despair arrives
And knocks on my door
It's only You Lord
Who restores faith to my core

BLESSED

After another trip to the emergency room for pancreatitis, I was feeling a bit worn down. When I arrived home, I was so thankful the pain was gone. God gave me this poem. I knew, and have known, no matter what happens, I am blessed.

May God be gracious to us and bless us and make His face shine upon us. Psalm 67:1

I am blessed to be here
And blessed to say
I am able to be home
And live another day

I am blessed to have friends
Who love me always
Who serve the Lord
In so many ways

I am blessed to have God
In control of my life
He who comforts me
In any of my strife

I am blessed so blessed
To be given salvation
Though I do not deserve it
I receive it with elation

CONCLUSION

Although this was a difficult recovery, I was blessed by God through it all. I had so many prayer warriors lifting me up and I could feel it throughout the recovery time. Even when I was discouraged, I felt God's presence. I hope this book gives you hope in whatever you may be going through!